his mate) reckoned he
was the best English
poet of his
generation
love
Lesley x

TIEPIN EROS

TOM PICKARD

Tiepin Eros

New & Selected POEMS

BLOODAXE BOOKS

ISBN: 1 85224 130 6

First published 1994 by
Bloodaxe Books Ltd,
P.O. Box 1SN,
Newcastle upon Tyne NE99 1SN.

Bloodaxe Books Ltd acknowledges
the financial assistance of Northern Arts.

Cover printing by J. Thomson Colour Printers Ltd, Glasgow.

Printed in Great Britain by
Cromwell Press Ltd, Broughton Gifford, Melksham, Wiltshire.

Almost every desire a poor man has is a punishable offence.

CELINE: Journey to the End of Night

The ornaments of the Proud are from the bowels of their betters.

CHRISTOPHER SMART: Jubilato Agno

Inclosure came and trampled on the grave
Of labours rights and left the poor a slave
And memorys pride ere want to wealth did bow
Is both the shadow and the substance now.

JOHN CLARE: The Mores

Acknowledgements

This book includes poems from the following collections: *High on the Walls* (Fulcrum Press, 1967), *The Order of Chance* (Fulcrum Press, 1971), *Hero Dust* (Allison & Busby, 1979) and *Custom & Exile* (Allison & Busby, 1985). *Dancing Under Fire* was first published in *Poetry Review*.

For the new poems in the first section, *Tiepin Eros*, acknowledgements are due to *Antología del Festival Internacional de Poesía de la Ciudad de Mexico, The Bulletin* (Australia), *New American Writing, Poetry Marathon '93 Charity Anthology* and *Rimbaud Centenary* (Plymouth Arts Centre, 1991), and to *The Shadow & The Substance* (Channel Four Television, 1994).

My thanks are due to various editors and publishers over the years, including Stuart and Dièdre Montgomery of the Fulcrum Press, Clive Allison, Margaret Busby and Bill Swainson of Allison and Busby, Ric Caddel of Pig Press; also to Eric Mottram.

This book is dedicated to Joanna Voit, my family and friends.

Contents

TIEPIN EROS

Dedication

you took something
that wasn't mine to keep
or lose,

and that look
does not suit the inside
of my wallet

I'm always pinning
your pictures to the wall
or writing you a letter

slipped between sheets
and other readers

it's the only place to be

Sea Trout

Sharp shadows slice
through silvering shallows.

As a keeper's car cruised past
I crouched beneath a storm-felled bough;
sheltered from the torrent
and hidden from the road above
I dropped the stick I'd slit.
What I needed was a forked branch,
a deniable tool.

Charging spurting currents
in lightning-coloured skin,
the abrasive flesh ripped
from my slipping grip, then
my bear's claw gaffed it
from the knifing syke.

Pith of the river, sand dancing
in precipitous water and berserking burn.
All muscle snaking spine and slapping gut.

It is as if they want to be still
like the hills they leap into –
thrust up in volcanic waves
where the beer-clear waters start –

to spawn their amber rain
in the ocean tasting mud
of their beginnings.

A History Lesson from My Son on Hadrian's Wall

On the edge of empire
running vallums along their arteries
keeps the generals off the streets.

A snake on the blade
said the man from the military museum.

What does a snake say?
He does several side steps
then strikes. *A perfect symbol*
to engrave on a sword.
And a dangerous weapon
in the hands of a Roman soldier.

The camp legionnaires wore enamelled armour
made by smithies sniffing mercurial fumes
from boiling quicksilver.

Everything is thinned and silenced suddenly
save for tree-topping Tornadoes
flying under radar.

Can we go to the pickets museum?
When were the Romans born?
Who were their mothers?
How does life begin?
Is my grandad dead?

The dig at Birdoswald fort,
sponsored by British Nuclear Fuels Ltd
is searching out the grain store.

Overlooking the Irthing
a stag in the gorge scatters
at the noise of our race
to the edge of the precipice.

As I ran out in front he said
the first one there loses.

Energy

The swallows on the TV aerial
face west and watch
the fellsides undulate
like dunes in the dusk.

They gather on the telephone wire.
Yesterday, fifty.
Today more than double that.

Quick clouds skim purple
off the fells.
These are the facts
I'm faxing down my line.

Slow flying jets under
a low lying sky.

They fly south
over armies assembled in the dust,
appear on radar screens
in the shape of cities,
disperse, with grains of sand
in a storm.

A Casualty of War

(in memory of Mieczysław Voit, d. 31/1/91)

Forgers of electric flags
inflame TV desert sands.
The inside of my glasses
spray with salt.
I will not wear the black.
I'll keep awake
and hear the breathing boards
inside my room,
the traffic on 6th Avenue.

Sobbing, my heart,
oceans apart from
all your hearts,
where his heart stopped
though still
still beats in you
and in our son
beside my own
and yours.

My night is over yours
has just begun.

The Double D Economy

Depravity and Deprivation

Back of the pub a rottweiler
ripped a kid's throat out.
Nanny broke baby skulls.
5 a.m. phone calls.
Hello?

There is no response.
The internal phone in the DSS
isn't working.
They only listen when you think
they aren't.

If there was a riot
I would have joined it.
If I had a machine gun
I would have shot it.

Fuck Kung-fu all at once.
Can't come against it hard on,
you'll just leak all over
the shatter-proof glass.
Got to pour your outrage in a bottle,
light the fuse and throw it at the

right moment,
in congenial company.

Or join the guerillas
for a pair of boots.

Meanwhile who's for dinner?
Eat leather.
Lick hockle off the trough.

Come joins us.

Who is the Whore of Armageddon?

Who sucks milk from baby mouths?
Whose breath is bilious with unemployed bombs?
Whose ulcerous pout is the stokehold of a prison ship?
Whose legs are knotted with varicose veins
from standing on the necks of health workers?
Whose palms are greased like a money-box in a fuck-factory?
Whose voice is a massed band waltzing the last post?
Whose tongue is gang warfare on a global scale?
Whose grammar is a tattoo of paratroopers
tap-dancing on teeth?
Whose brain is a thinking tank?
Whose eyes are internment without trial?
Whose smile is manicured money talking?
Whose arms embrace the globe?
Whose shadow is the smoke of multinationals
chasing cheap labour across continents of new markets?
Whose supermarkets are full of hungry thieves?
Whose police juggernauts deliver riots
to experimental neighbourhoods with disenfranchised communities?
Whose television is programmed by corporations
in the government business?

A Public Relations Coup

June ninth nineteen eighty-three
we are told to expect
the re-election of missus Thatcher.
Three black men hung in Johannesburg.

June tenth the first letter of congratulation
snapped onto the mat of number ten Downing Street;
from the government of South Africa.

Hang it all, said Dennis, lifting the sneck,
you can trust them to play the white man.

Drip Feeding Norman Tebbit

Letter to the editor

I blame the media for the current outbreak
of unprecedented copycat patriotism:
there's not a disc-jockey or newscaster
who doesn't refer a dozen times daily

to the delinquent spending of untold thousands
on the forthcoming so-called *Royal Wedding*.
They flagrantly encourage those layabout elements
in their ram-raids on the public purse.

There is a clear connection between
media coverage and new outbreaks
of this dangerous social disease.

Last Friday I watched a BBC team
instructing viewers in
the organisation of *street parties*.

It's all very well to claim
spontaneous outbursts of feeling,
but let us be blunt and not monkey about,
a campaign is being directed by inside agitators.

Feckless people are being manipulated
into adoration of parasitic elements.
It must be nipped in the bud
before it is too late.

If it cannot be prevented I hope,
when the so-called *wedding* takes place,
the police will use water cannons and gas
to clear the streets of those yobbos
emulating what they've seen on TV.

Let's picket-out this scab summer, sun

Miners' Strike 1984-85

half moon
          over Camden Town
I run amongst the
apple stalls
          and broken homeless
seeking green fruit
the colour of your eyes

I want to lick
your spit kisses
from my lips

crossing the picket-line
is an act of violence
for money

the colliers
and their families
stood silent in Fleet Street
to remember their dead
so many
          and so silent
between Holborn
   and Ludgate Circus
      banners draped in black tags
flapped
      as they stood, silent,
so silent,
   to remember their dead

What Did It Say?

She said *I've posted a letter,*
you left lying around.

I couldn't remember who to.
Was there a reason
it should stay in the house

unwritten maybe
as well as unposted?

Who will open it?
What will they find?
Did I sign it?

Was a slow delivery meant for it?
Would there be snow on the hills
Slush in the gutter?

A bullet knows its target
letters get lost
arrive at the wrong destination.

Would the recipient reply?
Will it cost me?

It already has, too much,
and the engine ticking over
in the street outside.

What Maks Makems

an icy wind bites
through stocks
whipped-up
from the Wear
where shags in a frozen
dive
break black water

a crick-neck welder
bent
beneath the boat
with his head in a mask
burns her together

he crawls
in a double bottom gutter
beneath the engine room
tank-top
to the sump
where the clatter
and rattle of caulkers
shatter the ear
drum running shudder
of a bulkhead drop

the only way out
in a panic
is backwards
over
an extractor pipe
and cables
through a hatch
got smaller
in a swollen flap

the Makem can
weld himself into
a steel box
and seal the lid on
afterwards

Ship 1431

(26th March 1986)

born
at the ship's launch
on her waxy stocks
slipping down her belly
on hand-greased oak blocks

Spring on the river
and a blizzard blowing
welding all day
on a waltzing cherrypicker

sleepless eyeballs skinned
sandblasted by flash

the director drunk
whipping up waters
chopping jobs

her bulbous bow
bends tank-rats double
knocking off dogs
in the double bottom

a shipwright all over
and under
checking
tucking her in
shoring her up
to slide her down

shot-blast gritting
the greased wax-ways

born my son
along her butts and seams
drag chains
in a quick cloud of rust

Contractor Song

be a casual, take a chance
what have you got to lose?
an eye or an arm or a severed spine
and brother, your right to choose

so shut ya trap and divvin fight back
when the rigging is insecure
fall off a plank and draw a blank
and sister you'll work no more

don't give no shit to the management prick
when you're in those double bottoms
but learn to lick his contract stick
your union rights forgotten

so shut ya trap and divvin fight back
when the rigging is insecure
fall off a plank and draw a blank
and brother you'll work no more

don't take the hump in the engine sump
when you weld that deep thin seam
or start to cough, the extractor's off!
did you hear your marra scream?

so shut ya trap and divvin fight back
when the rigging is insecure
fall off a plank and draw a blank
and sister you'll work no more

your lungs are full and your senses dull
but try and think of when
you had some pride stood side by side
with other union men

so be a casual, take a chance
what have you got to lose?
an eye or an arm or a severed spine
and sister your right to choose

come on me boys put doon your toys
and bring the union oot
to protect ya pay and the family, hay!
you'd better friggin shoot

don't shut ya trap you must fight back
when the rigging is insecure
or you'll draw a blank when that missing plank
means you'll work no more

A Room for Shelter

We doss on a mattress
from floor to floor
to be together.

Her belly pained up
and burnt with the babby.

She had it cut oot in hospital
and lost three pints of blood.

Me and the little lad
stayed in the damp gaff
till they came back glad
in an ambulance
and the winter in our room.

The kids' clothes stay wet, but.

Cowboy Is King

Cowboy collected empty beer glasses and bottles
and took them back to the bar counter.
He spent most of his time doing it.
Young blokes mocked.
– *What did you do in the war, Cowboy?*
– *Won a medal.*
The jukebox brayed a bar full of grafters.
A dole-wallah made a half pint last.
A dull, dark, wet Saturday.
The bar smelt of sweat and damp dust.
A squad of brickies came in and ordered dog.
They stacked up bottles and drank them fast.
A thick-built jock scoffed.
A man in black asked for the crematorium.
– *The beer's not that bad.*
Everybody laughed except the Scot.
– *I don't think that's funny.*
– *Fuck off, Jock.*
– *Make me!*
The bar went quiet. Billy tried to bop him.
An older bricky blocked the bother.
– *Leave him, he's a nutta.*
He curled his thick fingers into a brick fist.
– *Piss up ya kilt.*

Jimmy Shand and His Band played a reel.
Two old women linked arms and danced;
one of them wore nylons down to the ankles
and a foot poked through her shoe.
A young bloke with brylcreemed black hair
linked arms with his mother.
They sang a Tom Jones ballad.
Her stained raggy brown coat rubbed
against his new made-to-measure suit
with snowflake shoulders.
She gripped his wrists with her bony fingers
but held him with her wet eyes
as she mimed the words.
The jukebox jumped and jacked up the jock.

– That pile of piss can't shaft me,
I'll stick him like a pig.
A glass shattered.
The brickies got agitated.
Billy, on bail, backs off.
Cowboy grabs a handful of bottles by the neck
and dumps them on the bar.
Dead Admirals he calls them.
Sixty, flabby, no teeth,
and a para tattoo.
– I wish you'd pagga that plonky, he'll
get Billy banged-up again.
– Will do for a dollar.

He shoves past the shoulder stacked bar.
– Oot the way, twat.
A young bloke takes the piss.
– He's like that Japanese commando
in the Burmese jungle.
Hey, Cowboy, the war's deed!
– It's just started.

The old wife in the woollen coat watched her man
splayed, feet spread, breath spent,
weigh a dart in his fingertips
like her once swollen nipple.
The jock kept snarling.
– Give that cunt a scud.

Cowboy crossed the room and smacked him
six inches off the deck.
Only gravity brought him back
on his back and bled.
The mess mopped off his sneck
with a wet beer towel
and a pool of blood left to paint
a legend on the floor.

When the pub opened again
Cowboy was wearing his World War medals.
Three or four young blokes took the piss.
He slagged them for their sloppy patter
words he used when they were flap-batter.
Secret words, barrow-boy words, gypsy words,
prison and police-cell words,
pit words, ship, sea and shipyard words
barracks and brothel words,
knocking-shop batta-splatta, pit-yacka,
alcy knacka, betting shop Yankee chatter.
Changing, spontaneous slang.
They screamed with laughter at his rage.
– Look, there's the fucking ketchup on the deck.
And I'll tek you, you cocky get.

The barman came across and pinned a paper
on the wall above their heads.
It said **COWBOY IS KING**.

John the Baptist's Redundancy Speech

let me bring you
my head on a plate

a dog to hang your hat on

the first telephone I find
with a pub in it
I'll give you a ring

giro permitting

Nues

(a painting by Djurdje Teodorvic)

two women in a crimson room
sleep naked on a large cushion

the redhead, left arm
over her lover's shoulder,

has a yellow cloth
across her crotch

their heads and nipples
almost touch

a Siamese cat curls at their feet

two red tulips in a jar
lick out their lush lives

the cat's paw flicks
lips in its sleep

her fingers under cover
of the yellow drape
in a yellow dream

warm breath her hair
and ear purring

through a dark blue window
or painting on the wall
a moon is just a blot of light

The Bridge

She stroked his shoulder
with her skirt as she passed
and put a beer on his table
without waiting for payment.
No one noticed, not even her boss.

When he bought another with a fiver
she gave him change from ten.
A rep grabbed for a shag,
but she shrunk the prick
with the lick of a smile.

He waited in a battered wagon
opposite the buffet window.
She collected glasses and
polished table tops with a wet cloth.

Brushed her hair in a mirror
between the spirit shelves
and ran lipstick along her mouth.
The gaffer counted cash
and made notes on the back of beer mats
which he stuck behind the till.

Driving through the drizzle-painted suburbs
the city fell away beneath them.
They parked under the bridge
and gazed at the black waters.
I've got thirty minutes before he'll miss me.

The heater lifted a yellow curtain of autumn air
as they love-fucked with their clothes on
in the back of the wagon, and the engine panting.
One long shuffling animal under a heap of coats.

With its abandoned factories
and shutdown shipyards the river
slapped its hips against collapsed wharfs,
idle slipways, skeletal staithes.

Tower blocks edged over the opposite bank.
Some windows dark and some lit:
a woman washing dishes and a man cooking a late supper.
Lights from a TV transmitted on a drawn blind.

He looked up at the bridge he'd cross tomorrow
going down south. Looking for a job.
Looking for a life.

I'd come with you if I could.

Verboten te meren

When Angie Baby
of Panama
getting a pull
off Eros
in the Nieuwe Maas
at midnight,

kisses,
her lips stick,
tasting a tongue-cup
of come.

A Tale of Two Hats

(Adam Willaert)

behind the silk ladies
and commanding burgher
who points with a stick
to a large cod
writhing at the feet
of a fisherman
tipping his cap

a woman
pulls at the arm
of a drunk
puking
into his own hat

others
fight and fuck
by the water's edge

Diana at Her Bath
(Rubens)

Diana,
her nipple
kissed pink
by the red dress
so recently removed
and rolling
the low light along
its narrow folds,
slips off
a white silk shift
and traps us
in the act
of seeing.

Portrait of a Widow
(Abraham Lambertsz van der Temple)

The young blonde widow
in the black velvet dress
whose unsprung curls
spring around a string
of rolled spit pearls
holds a white peony rose
as though it were a fig leaf
just plucked from Cupid
who now stands naked
behind her

De Kwakalver
(Gerrit Dou)

a baby has its arse wiped
next to a charcoal fire
where herring bake

carrots
red and white cabbage
shallots

still-life
delivered on a wheelbarrow

Ford in the River
(John Baptist Weenix)

only a dog
caught cowering
mid-crap
centre canvas

and a boy
with his mother
who picks a stitch
in her skirt

look, direct
and vulnerable,
towards us

the rest
on white war horse
or driven ox
pass by

A Bar in Rotterdam

Rita pours *geneva* with a smile,
tips the bottle from its bottom
and breaks ice cubes apart with her hands.

She is known in Shanghai, South Shields,
Szczecin, and Tampico
and is shadowed by a bearded sailor with a pot belly
who plays a one-armed bandit next to a poster
for Frosted.

Angel, wearing snakeskin high heel boots,
rings the bell and buys us all a drink.

My name is Angel but I'm not.
The other bars have expensive girls
who make you feel good, but wake
with a hole in your wallet.

The beard with the beer belly takes the hump
and hits the one-armed bandit.

She has a weakness for new herrings
(and fresh sailors)
and gives me one from a white kid handbag.

On a Dutch Beach

Breakers belly and swell.
As she turns her head, afraid
of a moonlit lighthouse tower,
the swollen tide tugs at her hips.
She grips a wave-thrashed post
to push her patulous cheeks
into the face of a slapping sea.

A glowing string of broken sperm
clings to her floating hair.

Swimming through a galaxy of phosphorus,
stars drip from her arms and dissolve:
whole new constellations ripple into shape,
and break.

A New Jersey Legend

Joel Lewis told me of Fatsy Patsy
who shat his pants
and chased after buses yelling
HEY PINKY!
His mother wiped his arse, slapped him
into a suit and took him to a club
called The Edge
where he played fantastic piano
and made good money,
until he got off the stool
and started shitting around again.
HEY PINKY!

Lament for the Telegram

these short nights get longer
without you

The Perfect Polish Woman

stands simultaneously
in four different queues
while cleaning the home
and making stews

The Ommissar

never ask the same guru
two questions

Bugger Bupa

in America
the medicine looks so good
I want to get sick
and try it

Friggin Larking About

did you rub cowshit on your face
to get those rosy cheeks?
or just stand, in short pants,
jacking off behind the stacks?

The Sayings of Chairman Q

I am the true way sayeth the queue.
The queue is autonomous and non-aligned.
The queue has no colonies.

Queues face forward.
The person behind is always too close.
Frottage in queues for cottage cheese is common.
Stay close to the person in front,
let none come between you.

The queue is a way of life.
The queue is life.
The only good queue is a dead queue.
Leave with a full bag and the queue hates you.

Mutiny on the Queue.
Moby Queue.
Gentlemen Prefer Queues.
Travel agencies arrange package tours of queues.

The queue is immobile.
The queue is always right.
A short queue can be very long.
When the queue moves everybody moves.
There is a queue within the queue.
The queue hopes sweats is anxious and despairs.

Women get pregnant and have babies in queues.
Some become crippled in queues.
A cobweb formed on my wife in a queue.
People retire and have birthdays in queues.
Some queues have preservation orders on them.
Every queue throws up a leader.

The queue is the opium of the people.
Queues under the bed.
There is a queue forming over Europe.
If you reach the front and forget
why you're there, blanket buy.

FROM HIGH ON THE WALLS

(1967)

High on the Walls

strange to be higher
than a bird, to watch
them eat

when startled (the only
defence to be above)
take flight, and land
at my feet

Dusk

at dusk in Grainger Street
the starlings leaf the trees

they alight to the backfire
of a motorbike

Adultery

sitting in firelight
your face flecked in shadow

the little gold glint
of your ring

Coastline

sandcastles built to smother you
with kisses on the nose and lips

sandcastles spread across the beach
by happy bathers

crumble my turrets with your toes
wash me with your foamy sea,
make starfish my towers
while I bucket you with water

The bodies are touching

the bodies are touching
what is the matter?

where is your mind now?
what does it matter?

something is sleeping
where the mind wanders

it wanders away
let the mind stray

it gives back a pain
it sucks and is suction

the bodies are touching
                touching

Connie

tears sealed behind your eyes
soak away your mind

but last night, when I thought you were asleep
your head soft between my breast and shoulder
I was about to stream the pillows with your hair,
to submerge into your flesh, caressing with my lips
your swollen clitoris

            I felt a tear, and through the darkness
I could feel it shatter, streaming many ways

Me Your Ape

because you always wished for my silence
you said it did you good to hear my quiet

and I not knowing would make no noise
always wanting to say to you

you would be happy, smile, and wet your eyes,
I'd speak, and you'd hit me, hard, across the mouth

The Tongue

the tongue hollows caves for the lips
(a bottom lip stroked her uneven teeth
lightly as finger to knife)

the smooth soft surface licked
teeth touching teeth

Forbidden Birth

baby-juice
spluttering and bursting

I suppose inside is dark
because of you

your first sight the womb's first light
fresh with blood of you

they make her cover up
your little cave

I want to see you
all the time

I thumb her navel
and spread my fingers

To My Unborn Child

our heads met
when both of us
bent to kiss
your mother's cunt
you bent on parting her

I, pressing her closed
with my lips

found
you had been there
all time
before me

Bairn

you can't stop sleep, Matthew,
there's no shaking it off

each lash weighs a ton
and to keep apart
needs more than fun

pillows keep draughts off
as workmen leave geet gaps
in the cell

I tuck you in
your sweater's too small,
twice tonight you've sneezed

Matthew
hands of a newt
drums the box
and flutes

Puberty

(a painting by Edvard Munch)

don't creep away from my cock
        let's watch it grow
    let's sing songs
                to my cock
            & make your breasts bigger

        we'll unfold your arms
    & lie them akimbo

we'll uncross your legs
        lie on the couch
    and watch your hair sprout

Between Clock and Bed

(self portrait by Edvard Munch)

you knew old man
like Whitman

Painted like Steptoe
with striped bed
and cod's head

Pictures
of old rooms
partly furnished
and prepared
for death

Whitman became an old man
his poems no longer
          had vigour

His beard
made room for his death

Old Munch
shave your lip
and look like my father!

The Street Cleaner with his 18th Century Muck Cart

Must have been used for bring out your dead
giant Mexican hat wheels, no handles,
to be pushed along after the brush had done its job.

And the wheels make the same sounds on the cobbles.
An employee at the corporation yard, but smiles;
a flat cap, a boiler suit, but still that look
of the eighteenth century.

You would say an idiot smile, though I say
old turnips and blobs in his cart
with straw and broken glass are typical;
he is his own man.

Birthplace Bronchitis

The old men cannot walk up banks
without leaving brown hockle on the path.

They spend their days at pigeon duckets
watching tumblers and trains.

They're on the sick
and cannot leave their pain.

The thudding industrial hammer
is not much harder than the men it has made.

Our fathers are coughing up its grimy phlegm
and we will know the taste.

Stowell Street Corporation Yard

where workers are in nineteenth-century conditions,
surroundings, looks, and poses.
Foremen wear probably the same clothes (not overalls)
proud to be humbled by their superiors.

Their men work amongst the rubbish in lines,
shoving back, bit by bit, boxes
and all the other shit we put in our bins.

And next to the corporation yard a big new building,
while the men work with their hands and backs
as many generations of peasants in fields worked before them.

City Council Poem

The Lord Sheriff's gold chain
sparkles with the names
of hanged men

whose lifeless limbs
dangle and decorate his chins.

He has the honour
to be present at the scaffold
as his predecessors were.

Is it their heavy memory
which causes your official brow to bead

and your sloppy gob water
at such entertaining deeds?

You said, when I asked you
what your powers were,
that you could lock me up
if I caused some disturbance
in the town;
but who, proud pig,
if you chose to knock me down
would lock you up?

The Decadent Voyeurs

They pass factories and pits and poverty
in flashy cars and spit:
return to coal warm fires
which from the earth
those other men have ripped.

Nenthead

the lead long drawn
from the mines
and the miners dead

their deserted workings
are left like monuments

where the crag crumbles
and the murmur turns
the stone to sand

the ghostly trickle
of the syke
has washed away the silt

and a soul
poured into me

The Game Bird

As I walked across the fells to Hangman's Hill
a family of partridge burst from my feet,
the young half flew, half ran
their mother feigned lame.

Returning, the same family flap,
but this time I chased the chick
and caught her.

As I stroked her head she squeaked
and from the corner of my eye
I saw her mother, lame again
to tempt me.

My hand open she dived for the heather
and vanished.
I would have brought her home for you
but feared her death
and your sorrow afterwards.

The Widow

If you tell me I lack vitamins
from vegetables, so should eat more
and not feel depressed
I'll tell you its not vitamins I lack
but the love of my life.

Don't tell me I need Bingo
and the Darby and Joan
don't tell me I need company
to not feel depressed.
Without my Darby
you can forget the rest.

You can't give me the love he gave me
so forget your country air
and homes to convalesce,
I'd rather be here, depressed.

Gang Shag

canny bird owa there
sharrap man yi think of nowt but tarts

divin kna tho
wouldn't mine a bash arit

hoo pet can a tek yi yem?
am a big streng lad
al luk after yi

a kna ya not owld enuff ti suck a dummy

hoo lads he's scored
what's ya name pet
howay gis a kiss
gis a bit feel pet
di yi fancy a meat injection
well jump on the end i this

suck me plums
gis a suck off

yi comin for a walk wis
will gan owa the quarry
a knas a short cut

leave is alen

sharrap oral belt yi

grab a
gis a bit feel
pull a doon
lets have a bit tit
howay am forst

am warnin yis al git the coppas
sharrap oral kick ya teeth in

pull a doon
rip a skort off
hurry up an stuff it
am next
are man quick
stick it in the get
howld a doon
she winit keep still
a winit be a minute
gan on man gan on

are that's nice

howay well
it's me next

Shipyard

your eyes narrowed
when we kissed

rivets welded
into a ship's side

Scrap

hoo kid
fancy yasel?

aye
howay ootside

scrap lads, who's jumpin in?

kick ees heed in
gerroot yi twat
stick it on im
kick ees pills
boorim in the nakaz man
wipe ees face wi ya raza
smash the get

are nar thats noron
sharrap oral kill ya

twat

fluffy bum
puff
shite hawk

suck ees plums
boot im one
bottle im

here's a horny
the enamelled whore

scarpa lads

FROM THE ORDER OF CHANCE

(1971)

Put Britain On Its Back Week

Queen's Message

what's the marra wi yee?
give is a poke
yi want nowt but gobbles
am fucking choked

Advice to Young Poets

if your muse refuses
to tickle your balls
fart in her face

if she says *Fuck yourself*
take her advice
        and get on with it

the Arts Council
    is the home of contortionists

The Devil's Destroying Angel Exploded

        no sound
but horns of Southern ships
        and flapping wings

no colour
        but dancing black

producers of heat
        confused in the cold

moon full above the dole

        sleep children of chilled night
whose fathers were black men

        sleep bairns, shiver now
ya fathers' gold is stolen

strong fathers of a harsh past
        despondent now
slag faces rot against the dole

your hands held hammers
        & demanded much
the moment passed
        bairns curled cad in the womb

        you worried troops and churches
suffocated in the Durham bishop's stables
        when Londonderry's jails were full

        the coal you hewed
should have burnt them alive
instead you begged another shilling

        you should have thrown it
in their faces like a bomb
        fed your children joyful stories
                of the blood of those
        who cheat us

where we live
shattered smiles
break on haggard faces

manufacturers of filth
marry our wealth
in a confetti of votes

no breath of slum air

councillor, elected by my father,
he said you wore a worker's cap
called everybody *marra*
the word I heard was slave

bloodfluke in the brain of an ant
that gold chain scraped
from the lungs of pitmen

your gown is a union leader
gutted and reversed

look dozy fathers look
your masters have changed
drawn by the rivermist
you drift in a dream

ah father, your flesh is overrun with lice
and all your life you nurtured many parasites

Bunk

stars glitter
in the industrial valley
a ship's horn

lap   lap lap
drunk and huddled together
lap   lap lap
at the river together

            voices drift
mist on the river
        soft hair warm breath
my hands on your breasts
your dress unzips
    bare by the river together

lap   lap lap
huddled together

City Song

an engine's echo
clatters through the streets

bud of a rose opened
in my room overnight
before my mind
took account of time

drunks puke through iron gates

the call of bonny girls
whose echoes giggle
after gifts of love
from shadows
who share their loneliness
to taste their naked bliss

Murmurs

sleep explodes deep inside us

my fingers
become butterflies

strange words
travel to my balls

sensual animals move
in a swarm

of warm sensations

*

you come again this spring
throwing off black clouds
and sleet oppression

your familiar warm weather gestures
seem new

The Gift

the total of everything
is nothing
please take this gift
shadow of the poplar
on the red brick opposite

embryo
how you slip through
no shape
no name
no time to

we had been
in each other's dreams

how we build
and fall
and run

money
if you take all
take none

My Daughter's Heart

my daughter's heart beats against me
gulls fly up river
white factory smoke flows east
still winter trees

grateful for the crow's rough caw
so many sea birds circle the river
slow goods train

movement in the still trees
stray thought starling
co-ordination of all things
in a moment

Penny Blacks and One Pound Deals

Hey flea don't dig too deep
Pickard's brains are well scrambled
without causing leaks.

Stick to the scalp, lop,
and don't bite the same spot twice.

Listen nit, while I'm a joy-merchant
don't worry the punters.
If we meet fuzz, dance like fuck.

I'm getting to like you
but don't feel tied;
if you fancy new pastures
give me a knock,

I'll lean on a crumpet
and suggest a hump,
while you leap.

Rural Sex

fingers stretch across
whirlpools of ice

her black hair
and the water swirling

In a premature February warmth
a prancing pheasant sang.
In full-coloured plumage
he glints a sprig.

His first spring
and the sun sucks at his sex
like death.

He quails for a mate.

Blood beads cowp
from his beak

First Fuck

split she was
lay there two ways

shagged we had
and breast apart

one nipple fingered soft
felt like porno pictures
looked they should

fucked we had
and pissed happy glad

Refreshment

clear bubbles of joy
burst between us

come in our hair

a Halloween wind gust
of bin lids and cat howls

rips at The Ship
in at a twist of the Tyne

Willy Wank

A black jerkin,
   black as a doorway's shadows.
I stand there trying hard
to fuck a bird upright,
sucking at her neck
and fingering her twat.
She sniggers when I snap her bra.
   Then fuck! A bizzy!
What's your name?

   Willy Wank, I shout,
pushing spunky hands on him
and run.

Nora the Prossy

Nora the prossy's got pox
she lives in Pink Lane
never been the same
since she opened her box
to a pug named Tuck.

Coil Mistress

come wet belly
        shock of windows
fingers on a wineglass

thighs entwine
        crumbling walls
stale and still
        any unlit terror
possible

I drew two snakes
        took a woman's shape

in your hand mine
        in your eye mine
fire flame
        companion
sister sister mother daughter
        snake snake snake

New Body

as you saw my leopard's coat
I was a tiger

as you felt my bear's claw
I was a snake

as you stroked my cat's fur
I was a fish

as you built me a lion's cage
I was a worm

as you gripped mountains
I was a stream

as you crept tunnels
I was the sun

as you sought warmth
I was snow

as you expected thunder
I was calm

as you expected blood
I was stone

as you expected shape
I was air

as you looked
I was invisible

as you felt
I was near

when I appear
you tremble

THIRTY DIRTY SONGS
IN SEARCH OF AN OPERA

Cream of the Scum

It's in the net!
Not quite pet.
Hero. Pudding.
You stupid get!
What a good'n.

It's off his heed.
It's in. It's not.
He lacked speed.
What a farce.
Next time use ya arse!

It slipped off his boot
like a greased rat
up a drainpipe.

Hero. Guttersnipe.
Cream of the scum.
With a heed like that
yi should be hung.

Lovers, lovers, football brothers;
rejects, dejects, clowns and crakaz:
boot him one, in the nakaz!

He's on the floor.
Not anymore.
Get it back.
Give him a crack.
Lob it. Stop it.
Put the block on it.

Watch ya teeth,
his elbow's lethal.
He's trying. He's tripped.
He's flying.
Did you see him shift?
I'll buy him.

Lovers, lovers, football brothers;
rejects, dejects, clowns and crakaz:
boot him one, in the nakaz!

The Daylight Hours

song for dole wallahs

A hev gorra bairn
an a hev gorra wife
an a cannot see me bairn or wife
workin in the night

so go way mr doleman
av got something else ti do
than spen me daylight hours
workin for you

Yes aa am a songbird
an a song bird must sing
an you, oh mr doleman
you'll not clip me wings

So go way mr dole man
av got something else ti do
than spen me daylight hours
workin for thou

Grab ya job an ram it
in ya stupid gob
ad ratha gan to prison
than de ya stinkin job

so go way mr doleman
av got something else ti do
than spen me daylight hour
graftin for thou

An if aa gan to prisin
the world will git ti na
the walls of a prisin
isin strang enuf for wa

So grab ya job an ram it
in ya friggin gob
ad ratha gan ti prisin
than de ya stinkin job

Hunga

There's a pain in me stomach called hunga
it happens six days of the week
on Friday we gan ti *the social*
thi give us some money to seek
and to see some way of payin wa way
some way of payin wa way
fora day
some way of payin wa way.

> On Monday wi gan wi oot bacon
> on Tuesday wi gan wi oot meat
> on Wednesday wi gan wi oot breed
> on Thursday wi gets nowt to eat
> on Friday aa gans an aa begs

There's a pain in me stomach called hunga
it happens six days of the week
on Friday we gan ti *the social*
thi give us some money to seek
and to see some way of payin wa way
some way of payin wa way
fora day
some way of payin wa way.

> Av not got the money ti buy her new clothes
> av not got the money ti buy him some toys
> al not git me hair cut
> al not git a job
> ad ratha be skint than an industrialist's cog

There's a pain in me stomach called hunga
it happens six days of the week
on Friday we gan ti *the social*
thi give us some money to seek
and to see some way of payin wa way
some way of payin wa way
fora day
some way of payin wa way.

They send an inspecta
each day of the week
ti see if am lookin for work
but av get me coat on
an walkin the toon
forst tryin to borrow a short

There's a pain in me stomach called hunga
it happens six days of the week
on Friday we gan ti *the social*
thi give us some money to seek
and to see some way of payin wa way
some way of payin wa way
fora day
some way of payin wa way.

Brother Frank

I tried being swank
all I got was a blank
I think it's a wank
brother Frank

are we alone?
turning to stone?
or just breaking bones
I hear the moans
brother Frank

have you a clue?
I mean what to do?
here without you
sing me the blues
brother Frank

let's dance
let's take a chance
cause an avalanche
brother Frank

Scab by Moonlight

you aint the boot-licking kind
but should bear it in mind
when you get hungry
when you get hungry

you aint the black-legging type
but might give it a swipe
when you get hungry
when you get hungry

What Can You Do?

you wear a bowler hat and pinstripes too
carry a brolly and lunch till two
but all I got yes all I got
was a boiler suit bright denim blue

    what can you do
    what can you do
    with a boiler suit
    bright denim blue

my father was a railway man
and there he got stuck
squashed between the buffers
of two shunting trucks

    what could he do?
    what could he do?
    rub the grit out of his eyes
    turn his pick on you

mother was a charwife
used to char for you
kept your hands lily-white
hers needed seeing to
she washed your stairs
and scrubbed your floors
peeled her hands with *Flash*
while you were having menopause
riding on her back

    what could she do?
    what could she do?
    she could have scrubbed out you

Magistrate's Song

I'm a snob I'm a slob
I'm an upper-class yob
and I just can't get enough
of those working-class scruffs

I put 'em in a cell
and interrogate
I take 'em through hell
cause I'm a magistrate

I'm a snob I'm a slob
I'm an upper-class yob
and I just can't get enough
of those working-class roughs

A job would be a luxury
we can't afford to spare
Make 'em feel guilty
and indulge their self despair

I'm a snob I'm a judge
and I'll never budge
I love to see them cower in my mud
I'm a snob I'm an upper-class yob
and I like my kids rough
then I just can't give enough
of that disciplinary stuff
to those working class scruffs

I really like 'em hard
and I really like 'em thick
the thicker they are
the more we give 'em stick

I'm a snob I'm a judge
and I'll never budge
cause I love to see them cower
in my mud in my mud
then I just can't give enough
of that disciplinary stuff
to those working-class scruffs

DANCING UNDER FIRE

(1971)

Dancing Under Fire

love is just
love is just
love is just
a pile of dust

a narrow bridge
leads to a ruined castle
protected by wolves

a miner carved in stone
above his tomb
green
and black only now

taken from the Roman wall
to build instead of defend

to construct towers

others use one slab
at a time
to represent themselves

a blue fish
gave me your address
showed uncharted land
lay between us

walls were dissolved
one after the other
as we grew closer

owls of dissent hovering
only to preserve
that space between us

you were a dream
as I approached
withdrew

someone said
the instructions
were not meant
to be read

and understood

blackbird flew
to top of
sun tip
tree

all below
became dark
he sang

how the master race
longs to be enslaved
in the bedroom

slave
secured in his dream

hard
no wind
nothing changes step

love
flesh and faith
alone

a fixed gaze
burns into life

drums beat
a retreat to the stars

a sinking flaming head
quenched in the darkness
throws light on the cycle
light dark light

holes drilled into city concrete
to fill with concrete
no crack uncovered
no gasp of green

a graveyard
gives a splash
of living colour

the victors thirst
for their own more terrifying defeat

what taxation and energy
is required to maintain it

how the people
beat their guns
back into chains

she

points out the attic window
to a dragon coiled
in the valley

tells me
street lamps mark the roads

and the roads
are old

I ask for words
and her hair ignites

brings in
the dragon

I ask for a weapon
she shows me bracken
to kindle its fire

black
and burning

her eyes

the soil we squeeze
makes coal
to give the fire
the wings we need
to fly

we shuffle through you mother
to our deaths
took our claws to build a nest
and whisper to each other

we've grown wings and fly together
leaving you the woven twig
that shaped the egg

blistering whore, made us wolves
and I, like the rest, danced round
ancestor burning

out of their tombs
out of the rock
into the air

tall lady in the dark corner
take off your hat
we're in possession of a dragon
and it lights the room with fire

    wind blows through
    the windows
    flicks the trees

    glittering of stars

tonight we travel the passageways
and tunnels
all is dark and warm

movement becomes peace

curled in my womb
burn with flames
that give no light

    little black flame
    in my little black belly
    little black flame
    in your own black belly

a train rumbles
in the valley

dream of dragons
roaring in my belly

the voice that speaks
is clear
my own
falters

whose head
is this
I gnaw
to a bone?

secure and sealed off
in my womb
answer one word

cannibal cannibal cannibal

what flesh there is
is yours

cannibal cannibal cannibal

that hand you feel is yours
those words are yours
the air you breathe is yours
the walls you touch are yours
and impenetrable
shaped into a shell
windows of darkness
walls of darkness
your teeth cannot crack rock
doors of darkness
leading into darkness

the sleeping sun
a pea skin your strength
the only nourishment
your swollen tongue
eat that
and stay alive another hour
but lose the power of speech

dissolve
reduce to cotton wool
and still dissolve

dissolve to white sea foam
and still dissolve

dissolve to fishes in the sea
and still dissolve

dissolve to eggs on a leaf
and still dissolve

dissolve to fibres in the roots
and still dissolve

dissolve to salt
and still dissolve

dissolve to blood
and still dissolve

dissolve a kiss
and still dissolve

dissolve a tongue
and still dissolve

dissolve a lick
and still dissolve

dissolve desire
and still dissolve

dissolve into her warmest fur
and still dissolve

dissolve the air
and still dissolve

the river's voice
is many flamed

Always shook. Always trembled. Always walked.
Marta from Westerhope.
We called him Marta, and he always shook.
They said he was shell-shocked.
No one knew him. He always turned up.
Sometimes twice or three times a day.
No day was complete without Marta.

We thought he was a spy or wanka.
Wore a slouch hat and rain coat in all weather.
If yi gan to Kenton Woods,
Marta'l getcha, Marta'l getcha.
The more we discovered of the world outside
there was Marta. He was no joke.
Silence when he passed.

Great stories followed him:
Hero! Raper!
His fingers trembled, his eyes blinked,
pulling the hat over his face.
Watch out for Marta!

Got red hair and walks all day.
The large world must seem small to Marta.
A hush round the lamp post when he passed
into the next lamp's light.
Hoo, here's Marta, looka!

Tall and thin. Speaks to no one.
A ghost from another age
with bombs and trenches.
Mustard gas and Marta.
Steel helmets and Marta.
Bayonets and Marta.
Medals and Marta.

one two three
one two three
marta'l getcha
on is knee

four five six
four five six
marta'l tak
doon ya nix

seven eight nine
seven eight nine
martaz name is
frank en stine

Tot from the shop
said a bomb exploded in his trench.
Comes in every day for Woodies and matches.
He has no words. Only demands
and memories of old commands.

marta's got a blade
in his mack
marta wears an old
gas mask

marta got a shock
in the war
marta he can't fuck
anymore

marta's got no cock
in his pants
left it on the shores
of france

He wasn't anybody's husband.
Not that we knew.
He lived somewhere else.
Motherless Marta. Left her
with his enemies and memories.

Similar to Himiler, only he'd
never been in the Albert Hall
and his balls were used as anchors
for his cock
to stop it floating off like a Zeppelin
every time it sniffed fresh air.

Marta,
do you get your dole on Fridays?

a train replaces the dragon
roars in the valley
engines shunt

a voice from someone's telly

oh you watch me
on the box
my lips move
my eyes are dots
my tune is an electrical cackle

wired voodoo
in a wooden box
I am a coffin
with a window

you can watch
see me flicker
if you touch
I will shock

it's not electric
interference
that makes me present
shadows
of the real event

I am rich
I am greedy
pay the rent
and I will give you
anything I invent

my hand to her breast
tore away the cloth
as her foot touched my leg
ran over a field scattering birds
smelt the damp grass
blood to a gallop
peewits flash their white bellies
my fingertips exploded at her tits
a rabbit dashed to the stream
gull white and wisely perched on a bridge
cocked its eye at a fish

her nipple filled my mouth
whisper silver fishes

one touch could crumble

Edvard Munch's soul
stirs in her womb

with no glib intent
lay my head on her belly

she licks my ear

we love
a little

father you built the lines I travel on
my direction was laid by your sweat and death

glitter magpie
take my soul and squeeze it
set your beak and tear it out

a hawk in the railway yard
I saw it snatch a prey

peck a hole in the sky
let the magpie through

boats sail cities on secret canals

what is chosen
remains

FROM HERO DUST

(1979)

Bonfire

dragons disperse tonight
like split mercury
amongst the houses

children crouch
round an alley fire

make rings
with glowing sticks

black face Michael
stretches across two
well-chewed bits
of gum and
peers down
a manhole

his jumper sparkles
with drizzle

Gateshead Mammals

sea monsters chalked on the asphalt road
stride the alley
as though it were a long cave

we sit half way up the pyramid
to our back door
sun sunk in the coke works

mammal bodies swim beneath the flapping clouds
which women hang in zigzag lines across the lane

there are beast with wings in the cellar
beaked and mucky faces contemplate each other

the children have built a toad-run
we sit and watch the sun down

there is nothing else
to do

San Francisco Snake Dream

the skull masks
    my children wear
fit better here

    fog horns
sound so clear
  in this still place

illuminated seeds
        burst in the city

siren screams
  re-echo
through the streets

broke my daughter's
        dream
  and mine
a snake
with thrashing head
    passed on to my son

we ended
    chopping it
to bits

Snake

a blackbird
sang
the sun

raised
towards it
balanced on my waist

she woke
we kissed
I've been bitten
by a snake
my tongue
hissed

Storm

surrounded by horses
heads shaking and rearing

I hold her small tit

there is no way past
legs thrash

Next Door's Bairn

waking at four to your cries
I've grown to expect you
with wall-shaking trucks

that simple cry of need

awake, hungry, your heart opens
and is filled

I count your howls through thin walls
when television and stereo cease

rain shuttles in the gutter

bairn   a singing star
quivering lark
over the roofs and slate drains

walls
and the need to break them

I feel your weight
suspended in my arms
your calls soothe and settle

awake and cry
my ears are tuned
and murmurs satisfy

thrush of tyres on the street

you howl
my typewriter snaps a beat

others hear us
through windows and walls of strange rooms
they tap their feet
some even move their lips
and speak

sing on and scream
I'll stay awake
and we'll assume the shadows
in their dreams

NYC

In a room of mirrors
a broken glass.

We dance.
What instrument are you?

A flash bulb
every three seconds.

Your hand on my knee.
My tongue in your ear.

If we whisper
they can hear.

Valentine

simplicity
say sleep

or
shall we
shower

have an apple

you are
as I need
water

shall I move?
do you dream?
shallow snow

flesh

melt this

Window

night machine
        and few survive

fierce tenderness

        dawn arrives
drawn in chains
denies flight to sleep
and none can sleep in flight

except a being
        born in darkness
whose heartbeats
                sound like feet
fluttering from foetus
        to wreath

        unwilling watchman
my ears piece each sound

        flock of seagulls
in a narrow cobbled street

who could release a woman?
or dream there was a key?

        her movements are her own
and from the shadows
        an ecstatic moan

        the city's turquoise mist
is scent of roses

summer sounds
are ceaseless

Hero Dust

saw the gypsy lady
told me all bad news
said I'm going on a journey
to the land of the blues

saw the gypsy lady,
said cross my palm with blood,
I'll tell you about your future
and it don't look good

1

an Aztec tunnel
under
the new urban motorway

    full moon
over the Victorian working-class houses

    a doll's arm
under partly demolished terraces

2

rusted wheels
cast iron cogs
chains poised taut
abandoned to rain
to sleet
    the memory of trimmers

a southern vessel nudges wooden staithes
    awaits trucks
shunted and unbuckled by teamers

    moss mottled with oil
and slime
    bedding for skeletons of scuttled boats
collapsed jetties

3

        played dominoes tonight
put down the wrong one and won
        threw the I Ching and got *Grace*
(it embarrassed Confucius)
        I'm confused

4

you threw me a glance and a rose
talked of riding through woods on a bike
        sent me a postcard of a Russian sun-god
and a peasant girl in ferns

5

a maze of streets
        and back lanes

four in the morning
        walking

cities reach unbroken
                to the sea

6

men climb ladders
descend pits
erect scaffolding
demolish buildings
devise plans
revise maps

sun streams through birch
spokes of your wheels alight

7

a cat howls
I dream of you

8

a gypsy surrounded by bairns
        she asks me to fuck

we are over-looked

9

this street is built with bricks
of furrowed brows
whole gutters explode
and tremble with sparrows

10

you may not find me kind
love has no hold on me

hold me

11

earth and a mutual glitter

12

to taste your lips
        I won't smoke
for a month

13

at thirteen I failed to become
        a complete teddyboy
owing to my mother's dark memories
    of Mosley mobs
she did not buy me a black shirt

14

fingers through forests

you come

a flower
shakes off its
pollen

each limb
trembles

15

it's cold
        I crawl up
and curl on you

16

this is the fifth night
        without sleep
I'm bruised with love

17

rats are chipping
        at the skirting board
birds are singing

it's dawn
I had to write a poem

18

hello pain
we meet again
lovely as before
and strange

hello sorrow
no need to borrow bliss
my lips lit
with your first kiss

why joy
am I your boy?
your latest toy?

19

play any game
choose the hardest pitch

dance on pain
keep sorrow in the ditch

20

I'm fierce
I'm furious
my fury flames furnaces
my fire flights hawks
my savage smiles ravage hyenas
my dreams devise daggers
demand death

my lascivious laugh

21

oh in she rushed
      flushed
with stolen roses

22

barefoot on broken glass
shattered mirror

this side of reflection
chandeliers explode
walls become walls within walls

follow this maze:
          this way out
          is that way in

'Withershins: a direction
contrary to the course
of the sun'

23

your beak breaks
    the flesh of my breast

I scream
tormented by dreams

24

moon
    full on the sea
what waves there are
what tides

your eyes
wide
as a mother's thighs

25

a hot animal lies beneath my hand
her ribs take the weight of my fingers

she wears her scar like a jewel

26

I hear her whine in the wheels of a diesel
her body the aroma of nipped buds

27

in unlit Boilerhouse Road
    an astronaut on a moped passed me
I hid in Reservation Street

'you are lost in the maze of a dying culture'

    she too had joined the cavalry

I replied
it dies in your betraying eyes

28

'I have saved the bird in my breast'

David Riley

David Riley stands upon a small platform
beneath the banner ***JARROW CRUSADE***
in letters larger than a man's head.
The characters are made from their bodies.
The words are printed in the sky.

His arm is raised and says
        I will not be broken!
His mouth is open and says
        I will not be stopped!
His shoulders are straight and say
        We shall not bend!
His eyes are wide and say
        We shall not close!
His legs are firm and say
        We shall not buckle!
His feet are steady and say
        We shall not tire!

A small boy beneath him, hand on hip
a mask lifted from his face, him,
he too, he says so.

Travelling Fan

The train rocks
a ten year old boy
with glasses
and scraggy red hair
to sleep.

He counts the cooling ovens;
they're all around,
a forest of smoking towers.

His white bag with blue letters:
          Leeds United
   and in gold,
the champions!

Is that your team?
Aye! who d'you support, Newcastle?
I don't suppose you want to talk
about last Saturday!

I didn't.

A poem by Toms Raworth & Pickard to Ted Berrigan written during a train ride between Amsterdam and den Hague in pursuit of a Polish visa

anywhere
is a bad place
to be stuck

Short poem describing its long title written ten years later while walking through Regent's Park

a loppy crow
flies
nobly home

From the lost poems of Sherlock Holmes

a man with a horse and cart
howled a fistful of yellow chrysanthemums

I thought of you and bought a bunch

an abandoned tailor's dummy
upright in the gutter
with a ticket for parking

Homage

a willow
        warbler
in William
        Wordsworth's
garden
        sang

sitting in
        his
rustic hut
        I gave a
hollow laugh

        but
    she was
gazing at
        the daffs

Good Turn

a flock of gulls in a panic
their wings brush against your tits

smooth head parts your lips
black eye reflects an eye

death drops a seed and sleeps

Owl

almost
perceptible

warm breath
wings in my ear

Dipper

my head held
in your thighs
a warm flower
opening at night
a strange letter
sleep brings
music
a bird in
your bush sings

Domestic Art

on a white
cabinet

in our three
blued
bathroom

she has folded
over a glass dish
of abalone shells

a bright pink
face-cloth

City Garden

in a city garden
she took me to her side
now no other place
can I abide

round a city wall
we walked
saw names of men
and women
chalked
and flowers
marked their fall

in a city garden
she took me to her side
now no other place
can I abide

Vis-à-vis Visa

Wedding song

this pattern
we must learn
to live with
& love
each other

our days together
measured in advance
and stamped

but they
might learn
from us
and soon
as we
   this day
delighted dance
our own
and altogether
other tune

Gypsy Music in Krakow

sitting in an alcove
on the old city walls
a three-foot gypsy musician
plays a violin

his left leg
dangles
over his right
and his feet hang
far
from the ground

he sings
with a cigarette
in his mouth
broken lines
which complement the strings

his half blind eyes
flicker

magnificent music
issues from the
dwarf's misshapen frame

we stop and listen
amazed to witness
such easy skill
from so improbable a source

a woman, fresh from church,
rushes to push
pennies in his purse
as she might
with trepidation
kiss the foot
of the baby Christ

if he appeared
with such a moustache

White Room

the street outside
is quiet with rain

in a white room
I stroke your long back

hold my shoulder
you sigh and yawn

opening your eyes
to another morning

White Rose

you gave me a white rose
put the lamp on the stove
it caught fire
the I Ching said
thunder above the lake
lightning in Baker Street

switched on the cooker
and blew a fuse
blue flash
you see
the whole experience
is electric

Jewish Cemetery, Warsaw

I walked in a wood
which did not sing
and a songless silence
hung deaf in my ears

the dead grew roots
held their bones tight
trees smashed packed earth apart
growing higher than the murder camps
higher than the smoke from living flesh

the dead here will never rest
their fingers rattle
in the wood's twig twisted top
where two solitary hooded crows
have built a nest

I walked in a wood
which did not sing
and a songless silence
hung deaf in my ears

Whorl

The women
          selling gladioli
on Nowy Swiat
   hold up
thrusting bunches
      of signalling
         colours.

She avoids red (but
when given them
as gifts
   quickly re-gives
to fresh guest)

cutting
      frayed inches
from the otherwise
      taut stalks

and plucks, daily,
   into her palm,
with three fingers
   and the heel
of her thumb

the dead
      and withered
calyxes.

In Search of Ingenuous

opening a dictionary
between *inflict*
and *inhuman*

my eye falls
on a flower
placed there
and preserved
by you

seeing
informs
my heart
infolds

*

between *idolise*
and *ILO*
a violet
whose moth petals
hover on
ignotum per ignotius

explanation
obscures the object

Warsaw to London Express

Half awake
from a rough night's ride
an old Polish peasant's back hurts.

He cuts pieces off an apple
which sizzles at the steel assault.

His big hands slice slivers of skin
with a knife which is a friend to him.

His familiarity with the blade
is ancient.

Passing me the fruit, he gestures:
to refresh the mouth.

On the edge of our seats
we gaze at the land.

With the confidence of dawn
he mutters.

Thick mist through dark woods.
Your scent on my scarf.

We roll slowly
over another border.

PS: Berlin:

Soldiers outside every unlocked door.
Legs spread, thumbs tucked
in gun-belt buckles,
like insolent cowboys.

Another leads
an unmuzzled German wolfhound
pulling on its chain,
as they search above
below,
and through the belly of our train.

I met a man

I met a man
with a human face
he was taken off a train
and replaced
at the border
hearts fell
like a rain of bombs
a wild bird broke in
and played berserk
in the lift to Stazewski's flat
opposite the *Muzeum Lenina*
there are three swastika reversed
and scraped into the paint work
knuckle sandwich
from one of god's mates
I met a man in a human place
who was taken off a train and refaced

Rat Palace

I got into trouble from the Labour Party
for saying the unemployed man did not have
the intelligence of a dog: when a dog is hungry
it takes food. Steals it. PADDY SCULLION

The ears are closed
snapped off and blocked.

How can we help each other?

Some lives can't be lived.
It's time to assume a more
rational perspective.

They punctured both his ears
and someone died.

Let's put a hat on all this
and head for home.

Where?

I gave a girl an atlas
and since they took away my passport
it's only a book.

Squires of the global village
give us prizes and prisons.
The telephone is tapped.
I hear a disembodied short wave radio
outside my window.
The guard dogs in Brixton are better fed
than the inmates.
Thirty per cent of prison staff at Wandsworth
are badge wearing members of the National Front.
Tax the dole, build more cells.

They are looking for volunteers to
collect the shit parcels.

I'm not one

These laws are meant to break us

some of the children were buried alive
and as they thawed
the earth moved like a field of corn
when they suffocated
the earth was still again

No News

We've been apart too many seasons.
Between this and the last breath
I have aged a millennium.
TV located in a corner of the living-room.
Someone is born and named.
We learn to live with the moments
not to despise the days.
The empire establishes another colony
of stateless terrorists.

Détente

a city in your smile
a continent on this tongue
an ocean on those lips

two falcons grasp a single branch
and flowers mouth their way through soil

the sun is out
and draws you through my pores
like sweat

I throw your picture down
and turn away depressed
return annoyed
confused

I want to run my lips
along your neck

I found a hole in my heart
and fell into it
there my children play
and make a *zamek* of my wounds
each day

another shape,
a heart complete,
grows beside the first
begins to drown the other
with its thirst

I stood between my two hearts
and both were beating

a swallow flew into this room
and banged against the window
I caught her in my hand
and felt her heart pelt
against my palm like rain

we were both held
her wide swift wings
in my anxious grasp

I wish to tell you about my prison

my fingers are the wings of god
his crushing love rushes through
their veins

it's blood that makes us love

Bush Telegram

bird chase bird
    through thicket leaves
we'll make love
    where earth bleeds

bird chase bird
    on desert sand
we'll make love
    in no man's land

bird chase bird
    on mountain sides
we'll make love
    where water divides

bird chase bird
    beneath a fern
we'll make love
    beside a burn

bird chase bird
    through burning grass
we'll make love
    and dance and laugh

bird chase bird
    from dawn to dusk
we'll make love
    till love makes us

Trick: Fancy Resistance

Shakespeare's
birthday

many happy returns
early morning
wolves bark and howl

spring winds
race through cages

what do tigers
dream of?

I wish you could see
your face
when you panic

roy rogers sings
oh give me a home
where the buffalo
and the deer
and the antelopes

you sleep with a dictionary
for a pillow

I am mrs tex
ritter

it's the real thing

I have a moon
in every pane
of my window

that's why you all smile
so much

you eat so well

restless

FROM CUSTOM & EXILE

(1985)

Miss You Miss Love

our love is a
flying bird
and each lost day
and night
is a feather torn
from its exquisite wing

for long
and graceful flight
each part
of its immaculate
plumage
should remain
intact

Shedding Her Skirt

I had forgotten
how to be
apart from you
and taught myself
tonight old tricks

should they have
their fusion?

colonise space?

the silence here
is different

a room
surrounded
by rooms

where is our
world?

are we in it?

noises all night
of sentences
I had forgotten

and in the remembering
forgot again

Sprig

of lilac
in a glass of clear water.

Hurry-along-ash,
always last to laugh,
touched green
by the sweeping dab
of a sable brush.

Two sparrows fuck,
delirious in a dust bath.

Stuttering primroses
on a south facing bank.

Dusk drifts in,
a slut in a loose blouse.

Early evening casts
long shadows on the grass.

Ok tree

Ok tree
        you can bloom
Spring's arrived
    with two green eyes

Portrait of a Woman Walking

pregnant, she stopped to look
at a boxer bitch
with dark nipples

not bad,
good shape,
no belly

balancing a blade
on her fingertip
she taught it
                to skip
and stick

chased swollen berries
in pricking brambles

the corner of her mouth
got stained with juice

I licked it off

Blue Brood

a high skied
        late august afternoon,
she sleeps:
    whispering
        (white clouds
blown from the west)
    of trembling leaves,
silenced

by passing trains
        travelling
nuclear waste
        along the track
to the coast

cumulus
        swells to
fluffy toys
        thighs
curled to touch
    her swollen belly
she listens
    to my heart
beating

her own
        is heard
by a third

I feel like
        a hen
hatching
        an egg

Signed and Dated on the Lover

(Ingres: La Grande Odalisque)

blue velvet november
bleached blue
bed and pillows

a peeled-off
burnt gold dress
still warm in folds
swells parallel
to her swimming descent

a blush of peaches
in a bowl by the bed

her arm
lies along her length
and tapers into
an enclosed palm
which smooths
a bone-handled fan whose
peacock tail-feathers flutter
flicking licks along
the inside surface
of her thigh

Goya Sketching Solona

She has a quick sensitive face
self-confident and alert.
I take notes,
like a policeman
loitering in an alley doorway.
We compare notes, and
they compare.

Solona Tired

She walks out of the room
but remains in the painting.

Come back tomorrow.

So you can take me
from myself?

Goya strokes shadows off
her lips.

Part of us is always lost
to another.

French Kiss

a ponce in Pigalle
   with an Italian blade
in his pants
      has a girl whose
smile slashes slices off
      the moon's face

a mechanical bird
   a negro sells
flies flapping
   in dizzying circles
like a street ballerina
   tap-dancing
a tango
   on cloud

Three for NYC

Valentine

so
soft
lips
amid
sky-
kiss
buildings
be mine

Offcast

crouched over
in a Bowery doorway
an old coat's forgotten
no one wears it
anymore

Spring

tall slow Sunday sunset
over the West Side Highway

walking down Hudson
thinking of you

two dogwoods bloom
in a doorway

Sweet FA

There's victory drunk and defeat drunk,
Relegation, league-drop and promotion drunk,
Board meetings and bent-manager drunk.

There's league table drunk
And cup drunk.
And World Cup drunk.
Finalist and semi-finalist drunk.
Newspaper and television drunk.
Hat-trick and soccer hooligan drunk.
Trainer drunk.
There's former star player turned pundit drunk.
Poor attendance drunk.
Shaking hands with Prince Charles drunk.
And winking at Princess Di drunk.
There's colour drunk and shirt drunk.

There's away game drunk and home game drunk.
Alcohol forbidden on the terraces drunk.
Referee and linesman drunk.
Offside drunk,
And half time drunk.
There's final whistle and injury time drunk.
Foul and player booked drunk.
Special cells and teach them a lesson drunk.
Short sharp shock drunk.
Stiffer penalties drunk.
Bring back the cat drunk.
Magistrates and mascots drunk.

There's right-winger MacGregor
dribbling in the press box drunk.
Mr Scargill and his 80 per cent minority
have moved the goalposts drunk.
Thatcher Fowling the pitch drunk.
Starve them into submission and call it a draw drunk.
Pickets police batoned and booked drunk.
Leon and his bovver boys in blue
sticking in the boot for Britain drunk.

If that sod left me in peace

It only lasted two weeks
then I couldn't stand the sight of him.
He knew I didn't love him
but he married us out of pity.
The Social Security made me take out a summons
for desertion. I told them
I didn't want a thing and glad to be rid of him.
They went mad in court.
But it's not his bairn, and I don't want his money.
I just want to be left alone.

The doctor gave us some pills,
but I get agitated and can't get done.
Then I get ratty with the bairn and think;
I'll kill him and there's nobody here to stop us.

I was lucky getting the flat.
But we've got rats from the deri' factories.
I found one on his cot. They come for the crumbs
and eat their way through a loaf.
The council put down poison.
I hope he doesn't find it.

He eats like a horse, the little get;
he eats more than I do.
Me sister said she'd take him
if her man gets a start down in London.
She thinks the world of him, mind,
and he'd be happy with her.
But I don't know.
If that sod left me in peace.

To my son who 'came out' at 16

the sky over Warsaw
        is the grey belly
of a snow bird,
        brooding

pigeons flutter
        past the window
like early flakes

a talking hedge-sparrow
        with a starling's
speckled shimmer
        said *hello*
and *compendium*

we worried about
        finding it a mate
neither too wild
        nor dull

winter trees
        by the river
like tongue-licked
        feathers

In Paradise

in paradise
I was ordered
to improvise

confident
of my co-operation
they paid in advance

it's the only sweatshop
in town

with a vacancy

Terminal Circuit

the grey-haired
        German poet
with a Lech Wałesa
moustache
   who switches his
vodka with
   my water
while falling
   over a table
shouts
CIA!
   and grabs
the French girl
   in red silk
pyjamas
   who takes my photo
with a flash
   as she
falls

Solidarity

          protesting
outside New York's
          Central Street Court
a black dissident shouts

free Amiri Baraka
   free Amiri Baraka

others
          hold up placards
saying
          no justice
in America

and

stop racist murders
in Atlanta

          one of four children
on the picket line
          gazes towards
a hot dog stand
          whose vendor
                    leans close
to hear the news

Carlo Crivelli's Saints Jerome & Augustine

Saint Jerome's red hat is held
by a long anchoring cord
to his navel.
The temple of god is balanced
in his hands like a toy.
A flash of light:
someone inside is vomiting blood.

Saint Augustine's jewel-encrusted fist
claws a crooked pike.
The papal crown is a galaxy of satellites:
precious stones in orbit
around his head.

A lion gazes in adoration
of its master: mane well-groomed,
teeth and claws bared.

Dissent is interned in temples.

A Sense of History

along the banks of the Tyne
to look for driftwood

dawn
mist over water
the great stone railway bridge
with blackened arches

a couple, pensioners,
– bent and stiff –
scrape the dry earth
with wire sticks

they hack hard clarts
collecting
small coal
slack almost
caked in frozen mud
and clay

Mutiny

Ted Berrigan & Tom Pickard. Spring 1982.

The admirals brushed
the dandruff off their epaulettes
and steamed on the *HMS Herpes*
towards Argentina.
I like doggies on their 'little feet',
don't you, I said. But they
kept rolling over, beneath the
tracer bullets and the
Atlantic moon, beneath the
daunting missiles and the Prince
in his helicopter. They were steaming
towards interesting places, to meet
interesting people and kill them.
They were at sea,
and it was also beneath them.

Ted's Old Man

Ted's old man had trouble with the company
and, as a point of honour and self respect,
died when they told him to go.

His old lady applied to a local party chief
who found her a job as a cashier
in the local school-meals cafeteria.

Ted said *come round, Alice is interested*
to talk and can remember folk's histories
a long way back: better than you could yourself.
It's scary man, when they end up in poems.

Just shout up at the window
and I'll throw down the key.

My Radio

its timing is perfect
and variable

its pronunciation
impeccable

its information
accurate

its sources
reliable

its correspondents
informed

its contents
incontestable

its motives
pure

it has many
voices

my radio
interprets the past
manages the present
and programmes the future

my radio makes truth
sound false

my radio is in complete control
and cannot be questioned

Dawn Raid on an Orchard

Pebbles skipping off the window woke me.
Throwing off light blankets, night
became an unmade bed.
Shinning down a drainpipe, skinned a knee.

Running soft in rubber shoes, trailing clouds of breath,
we knew that property was theft.

We wormed out where the wall was weakest
and found the broken glass on top was smashed.
Risking fingers and slashed feet we leapt.

The trees shook with blissful indignation
and we took ripe apples, tasting sweeter for the taking,
to fill our dads' redundant bait-bags.

A blackbird with a barbed-wire neck
cackled on a branch and clapped its wings. Flapping,
we dropped and lay flat as an alarm bell rang
in the gadgee's gaff.

Franky sprained an ankle, and pain suppressed his laugh:
we howled silent, afraid of an Alsatian growling,
a police panda prowling past.

His mumpy jacket zipped-up
and stuffed lumpy with knocked-off fruit
he limped towards the orchard wall.
From the inside it looked much taller.
One day, we said, *we'll mek it fall.*

Recipe: Pastime for the Unemployed

be mean with an onion
rip off its dried skin
and grip well

slice across its sphere
and chop

the onion will rise
into your nostrils
and speak to your eyes

keep slicing
weep and toss

into a hot iron pot
with chicken pieces

rib-tickling each
with bay leaves

use what herbs there are to hand
all spice chilli
cloves and yoghurt

decorate with saffron
sliced peel
from a fresh lemon

poke
with a fork

and don't let spitting fat
put you off

fight back

A Hole in Europe

One of two workers digging a hole
in a small square behind the old town's cathedral

is washing his muddy boots
with handfuls of water scooped from an icy pool.

A priest in black robes joins the diggers:
gazing down, as though granted a visa to Hell,
he hesitates, unable to afford the fare.

A gang of tourists arrives, wearing bright orange
waterproof clothing, and led by a guide.

This site of a monk's medieval graveyard,
has been disturbed often.
The surrounding houses were built for rich merchants
during the Renaissance.

A charwife washes her steps with a coloured cloth
resembling the national flag.

This hole was sunk by robotniks
who worked all night sinking wooden shafts
to reach a burst water pipe.

Pressing a thumb to his left nostril
he blows a snot two yards to the right.

Their drilling kept sleepers awake.
As you can see it is raining heavily
and snowing intermittently.

They drift towards the hole,
leaving the lecturer to guide alone.
Some take out sandwiches and vodka.

Followed by the priest and guide
they descend the frail wooden ladder.

The charwife covers the hole with her rag,
placing a heavy stone on each flapping corner.

Cell-Door: West-End Central

BB and DD were here
JAH LOVE
Horace snapped me stick
Budgie and Oggie Social Security fraud 83
kill spot checkers
Kings Cross Skins   Pat fitted-up
Jock The Fox Body Beef Animal
Jam Rider
Erika woz ere on warrant 83
Carol
from Cardiff
soliciting
PADDYS AND JOCKS
Taxi-door lugs Danny the dancer Tilbury Mods
Kevin=Jenny   Bounty Hunter
Gina I love you now and forever by Lorraine Pollard
you deaf twats open the door
Izabel is having my baby I love her always
Mick Falls Road Belfast
Geordie from JARROW near Newcastle-on-Tyne
MONEY TALKS
Anti-Christ Swansea Pete
Elaine Rogers 18.5.83 about ten past three I was
UP THE MINERS
Angel of Death
FUCK YOU
White Shadow
Jam Town Rockers   Diddy from Barnsley
LION
Raphael
PAPA ZULU
Dave The Rave

i waz glad you waz appy i waz mad again

Thirteen and a half hours without food
worse than Russia.

Chopin's Old Pianos

The Russians
          have thrown
from a third floor
          Warsaw window
Chopin
          's old piano

said Vice President
          -finger on the button-
Bush.

But
      in many of his
client states
          composers
are thrown
          from windows,
their shredded hands
          flapping,
pulped by rifle butts
   in football stadiums.

As a sign – humanity
   and love
of the arts –
tight security
has been mounted
   around
Chopin's old
   pianos

hooked up
          to the roof
in lead-lined
          bunkers
they hang
like carcasses
in a slaughter house.

Over dead composer cocktails
   and pin-ball holocaust
chess
         the banker generals
hear Chopin's
         music.

Stuffing wire cords
         into his mouth
they smash his teeth
   with piano legs,
punch fists full
      of splinter ivory
into his bleeding
         ears
   and anus.

Suspended
         by the tongue,
Chopin
         is pulped
to a mush
         with his
old pianos.

The music
      won't stop.

Skaman Report

Two letters from Lisa in Brixton

17 March 1981

I'm living in Brixton now
on the infamous frontline,
it's got hot water plus electrics.
I'm trying to find a job,
which is virtually impossible,
and doing 'A' levels at evening classes.

Most of my spare time is spent in pubs
and at gigs,
when we've got the money, which is rare
'cause the dole is only nineteen-fifty a week.

There's a huge rally for the unemployed
in Hyde Park next month –
with a load of good groups:
UB40, Specials, The Beat, Misty;
lots of Reggae and Ska.

In Brixton there's always a blues going on,
full of Rastas and spliffs. Great.

14 April 1981

None of the papers have got any truth.
On Friday this bloke got stabbed
so some Rasta phones an ambulance.
While they were waiting the cops turned up
and grabbed the guy to question him.
They dumped him in the back of the squad car
and kept him, bleeding, for twenty minutes.
Eventually his friends dragged him away
to take him to the hospital
and the cops tried to do him (and a few others)
for resisting arrest.

On Saturday they had loads of cops on the beat
and five or six vans of SPG patrolling.
What provoked all the trouble
was some undercover cops who,
after the police stopped a van and searched it,
started yelling and waving coshes.
The next thing was these blokes
pushed the police-van over and set it on fire.
I saw this just as I was turning the corner.
Then loads of cops with riot shields suddenly turned up
and tried to cordon off the area –
but crowds of blacks gays and punks
showered them with bricks and bottles.

Most of the reporters had their cameras smashed
but they let me take pictures.
One Rasta, who lives down the street, was saying
Take pictures of the opposition.
So I took one of six cops dragging
a fifteen year old kid up the street
and trying to bundle him into their van.
His mother was saying:
Let him walk!
but they wouldn't.
One cop whacked him round the face
so I said
Oy don't do that! but another cop said:
We've got to have our fun.

Then everyone was saying
Let's burn down the George, which is
a totally prejudiced pub next door.
Crates of gin and beer were brought out
and passed around the crowd (black and white).
The Rasta was saying
Don't get drunk!
and another bloke started collecting all the bottles
into piles
and started making Molotov cocktails
with petrol
from one of the many cars
that were later burnt.
Then they looted up the road
and into Brixton
where most of the jewellery shops, Woolworths
and some clothes shops
got looted and burnt.

Sunday was mostly people from outside,
tourists who'd read in the paper
and came to look.
There were twenty vans
and ten coaches of police –
and helicopters flying about,
so nothing could really happen.
I saw loads of fire engines and cops
up by the prison.
At one end they cordoned off Railton Road
at both ends,
so some Rastas moved loads of instruments
and mikes into the street
and started jamming.
Soon a street party was going.
One bloke was telling the cops to join in
and saying *black and white together,*
unite and fight together.
After about half an hour
the rioting started again.

I got a few cuts and bruises.

[Lisa Raworth and Tom Pickard]

Golden City Delivery Boy

a general's daughter
prepares roast lamb
in an immaculate kitchen

polished mahogany tables
   stand dressed
wine decorked
   waiters grab an early bite

between the Tower
and London Bridge
HMS Belfast
   meets the dreaming gaze
of an isolated banker
on the twenty-ninth floor

the young Winston Churchill
      is coming to lunch

delivering a selection of
   expensive delicacies
to the City Volunteer Club
   I joked to the manager

I've brought the pork pies.

Oh dear, another starf lunch
   he replies.

uniformed chauffeurs
in shades
rabbit on Bentley bonnets

Rothschilds
        Bank of America
Bank of England
        Bankers Trust

Lonrho
        seagulls' eggs
Camembert
    Brie

Kuwait Investment Trust
    protected by
bullet-proof glass walls
    which slide open
at a touch

Balls Brothers

the directors
    of the Bank of England
take a daily delivery
    of Port Salut
Sage Derby
    and dried fruit

when these gentlemen
    eat their prunes
and shit
    the pound will float
and we will swim in it

Spring Tide

(for Basil Bunting, Spring 1900 to Spring 1985)

1

A filthy winter to have lived through.
Dragged by the hair kicked and kicking into spring.

A year-long miners' strike,
broken.

Police road blocks blocked the motorways
and all roads leading to the north.

More reactionary than the thirties
the old fascist-fighting conchie told me.

2

While you lay dying in Hexham General Hospital,
we climbed Parliament Hill with our word learner son
to see the city from the lip of the basin
and to see the kites.

The little Geordie-Polak cried *keats*
when he saw the rainbow-winged mosquitoes
stringed against the cockney clouds.

You wanted sleep; a blood-clot
rushed to your brain. We pushed our faces into May:
snowflower our blossom told us,
thanking frothing hawthorn for the gift.

3

We stood by the North Sea,
a wash swirled around our feet.
Furthest from the shore
you stared towards a squall
on the dark horizon.

I warned against a threatening wave; swelling
it would overwhelm us.

Leaping to safety I glanced back and saw you,
steady, silent, still,
tracing the trajectory
of the wave's engulfing curve.

My son's warm hand on my leg
woke me drowning
in a cold sweat.

You, the dark spring tide,
and the spring
were gone.

mY peN

holds steady in my right hand
black, with a silver top
and tight gold nib

my **hero pen**
made in the People's Republic of China
and purchased in Warszawa
by my wild, cloud-haired, Polish wife
with apple-green eyes
and twenty faces

my **hero pen**
joins vertical strokes
to curved and looping horizontals
sucks noisy and quick
when dipped in black India ink

my **hero pen**
speaks slim volumes
running its incised beak
along prescribed lines

my **hero pen**
feels good between
finger and thumb

my **hero pen**
purchased in Dom Ksiazki,
on Nowy Swiat
where walls of books
are dripping ink
and threaten to flood whole streets

my ebony black, silver topped
Golden Star, Seven O Five
Chinese **hero pen**
looks good
with a blue and chrome
Three Seven One
YEUN CHANG –
made in Changhai,
comma,
China –
best quality,
swivel-type stapler
with four different uses

my pen writes adverts
for its comrades

my pen shouldn't get
too smart

My pen's ink
is the distilled dream
of fifty thousand million workers
weary with clocking-in
and clocking-out,
signing-on
and signing off:
enslaved to machinery
of industry
and state.

my pen refuses to recognise
obsolete forms of government
and votes with its feet

my pen wants to manage
its own affairs
thinking it knows best:

my pen demands
complete autonomy